Dr. T's Living Well

Guided Imagery

Dr. Richard L. Travis

Thank You for purchasing this book.

"Guided Imagery"

RLT Publishing   Copyright 2010

First Printing: 2014
Second Printing: 2016

ISBN 13: 9781494794408
ISBN 10: 1494794403

RLT Publishing

www.rltpublishing.com

INTRODUCTION

A Guided Imagery is a technique that is used to take you away into the inner recesses of your mind. It is a technique which, when mastered, can interrupt the stressors of the day, the compulsive worry, or just cleanse yourself of general stress. Using a Guided Imagery could be a part of everyone's personal treatment plan to promote self-expression, or speed physical or emotional healing. It is a good tool for everyone to learn to use on their own, or practice with a loved one. The benefits derived from using Guided Imagery are endless.

The word Guided Imagery is sometimes linked with similar words like Guided Meditation, Creative Visualization, Guided Visualization, Meditation, Hypnosis, or even Self-Hypnosis.

This is a book that leads you into the power of your mind to heal yourself, to change yourself, and perhaps to truly find yourself. Many opportunities lie within these pages for you to discover how to take charge of your life and make things happen, instead of letting things happen to you. This book will explain to you where, why, how, and when to do a guided imagery. It will also explain what may happen during a guided imagery session, and after. If you are a beginner, you are in for an amazing journey. If you have experience in doing guided imageries this book can add to your data bank of information that you can use to continue to grow.

There are several guided imagery scripts contained in this book which you could record, or someone could record for you. Affirmations are explained and offered for your use. There are also Links, TedTalks, and YouTube videos referenced for your pleasure and growth.

DEDICATION

This book is dedicated to all the people who wish to interrupt their negative thinking and replace it with positive thinking. This book is also dedicated to those who need help creating their dreams. Enjoy the journey.

Table of Contents

WHAT IS A GUIDED IMAGERY?

A Guided Imagery is a process. It is a process in which a person is guided through a creative mental trip using his/her imagination. A Guided Imagery is usually done with one person sitting or lying down with eyes closed, and following the instructions given by someone else who is serving as the "guide." (It is also easily accomplished by having a CD, DVD, laptop, or recorded app on your phone with the guided imagery process being played to the recipient.)

WHY DO A GUIDED IMAGERY?

The primary benefits of a guided imagery are relaxation and peace of mind, which are wonderful gifts in themselves. This is especially good for anyone who has little time to relax due to job, family or illness. So, the first benefit we notice is the release of stress.

Guided imageries can also help release limiting thoughts and emotions, raise self-esteem, help establish and meet goals, clear up questions needing answers, gain clarity, help heal relationships, and enhance physical healing. It seems that the usefulness of a guided imagery is limited only by the limitations of the guide and the choice of guided imagery script. Following are 3 uniquely different guided imageries you can click on, or copy into your browser, and get a feel for the different styles, voices, and messages.

https://www.youtube.com/watch?v=ar_W4jSzOlM "Ocean Escape (with music): Walk Along the Beach Guided Meditation and Visualization" http://www.bing.com/videos/search?q=YouTube+Guided+Imagery+&&view=detail&mid=D452936229B181A02E5BD452936229B181A02E5B&rvsmid=43E7467F8C1D6F240AF543E7467F8C1D6F240AF5&fsscr=-1485&FORM=VDFSRV **"10 minute guided body scan meditation."**

http://www.bing.com/videos/search?q=YouTube+Guided+Imagery+&&view=detail&mid=05589FAED1EA453F326905589FAED1EA453F3269&rvsmid=43E7467F8C1D6F240AF543E7467F8C1D6F240AF5&fsscr=-1485&FORM=VDFSRV **"Guided Meditation: Relaxation with Ocean Waves."**

BRAIN WAVES AND GUIDED IMAGERY

Electrical activity emanating from the brain is displayed in the form of brainwaves. There are four categories of brainwaves, ranging from the most brain activity to the least activity. The brainwave categories are **BETA, ALPHA, THETA, and DELTA.**

The **BETA** state is the brain wave frequency that we are experiencing when we are conscious. This is where we are alert, make decisions, make choices, learn, and process information. Usually we are in the Beta Brain wave state most of the day when we are awake. This is the brainwave showing the most engaged or active mind.

As we approach bedtime we begin to relax, and if we are not medicating with alcohol or certain drugs, we begin to slip into the **ALPHA** Brain wave state. Usually we are in the Alpha brain wave state the last 45 minutes before we go to sleep and the first 45 minutes after awakening. This is also the brainwave of relaxation and reflection during awakened times. Alpha brainwave function is associated with being in a peaceful state, like when walking in the garden or along the beach. During a guided imagery or meditation, we start relaxing and allow the brain to slowly leave the Beta brain wave state. The Alpha brainwave state is the state of mind in which you are very suggestible. That is why this is the state we reach when in prayer, meditation, guided imagery, or daydreaming.

An even less active state of the mind is when we are experiencing the **THETA** brainwave state. This is the frequency often associated with the beginning of sleep and REM sleep (dream sleep). As we go to bed and turn off the lights, we slowly slip from Beta, to Alpha, and into Theta brainwave activity. Some researchers have found that we can have insights in our

Theta state from dreams that we have. These insights can help us in our day to day life if interpreted and used appropriately.

As we slip deeper into sleep, we slip into **DELTA** brainwaves. The deeper we go into Delta brainwaves the deeper the sleep is and the fewer dreams that we experience. We cycle through all these brainwaves as we sleep, often every 90 minutes.

The goal of doing a Guided Imagery is to get into the highly suggestible and very relaxed state of the Alpha brainwave frequency. This is where we can use the creative parts of our mind to visualize peace, joy, healing, and anything else that we desire.

WHO SHOULD DO A GUIDED IMAGERY?

A guided imagery can be done by virtually anyone. It is not limited to adults or only spiritually oriented people. In fact, a guided imagery is not connected to religion or spirituality. It just feels uplifting, so people often feel that it is a spiritual experience.

A child can be led through a guided imagery to learn to relax muscles throughout the body. A child can also visualize himself being happy, successful, popular, and many other things. Children have much more active imaginations than adults, and therefore may be able to "see" more colors, more images, and participate more in the creative process of a guided imagery. Children usually love to do Guided Imageries.

Adults have more resistance to something new and must learn how to trust a person to guide them through a session of guided imagery. People who have suffered from abuse of any kind are even more untrusting of closing their eyes and following the direction of a guide. So, a safe setting, and a kind and understanding voice can really help these people.

The only adults that the author has had difficulty doing the visual part of the imagery session have been those who had abused a great deal of drugs in their earlier years. One way to test whether someone can visualize things is to have them close their eyes and describe what is on their bathroom vanity right now. Ask about the positioning of objects, the color and size of the objects too. If they can do that, then they are highly likely able to be guided through a Guided Imagery.

So, who can do a Guided Imagery? Virtually anyone who is willing to try it can do a Guided Imagery. The timing, setting, and topic to use are particularly important. Safety is also a major factor to remember. The author has always felt that complex Guided Imageries should be done in therapy, so that the person might have to "process" what they just experienced.

IMAGINATION

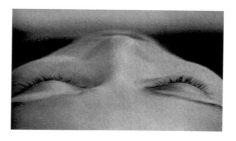

"The soul without imagination is what an observatory would be without a telescope," ....H.W. Beecher.

"Imagination rules the world." .... Napoleon.

"Imagination is the eye of the soul" .... Joubert.

"He who has imagination without learning has wings and no feet" .... Joubert.

"It is the divine attribute of the imagination, that when the real world is shut out, it can create a world for itself, and with a necromantic power can conjure up glorious shapes and forms, and brilliant visions to make the solitude populous, and irradiate the gloom of a dungeon." ....Washington Irving. It has been said that "imagination without action is pure fantasy." This statement suggests that it is possible to use our imagination to participate in the world in a way to produce a result.

In the early part of this century Emille Coue, a French physician, was faced with a severe shortage of medicine for the treatment of his patients. He introduced a concept to his patients that today we call_Affirmations. He had his patients repeat several times daily, *every day, in every way, I am getting better and better.* His patients had remarkable, if not miraculous healing using this affirmation. If we input this statement or other affirmations to

7

the power of the imagination in a Guided Imagery, then the possibilities for change and healing are restricted only by the limitations we may impose upon ourselves.

By learning how to use guided imageries, we harness the imagination. We can put the power of the imagination to practical use in private practice, and in our homes and hospitals. Today we have developed the left sides of our brain to a high degree. The left brain is the rational, logical side which we rely on to survive in our day to day existence. The right side of the brain is the creative side which, except for the more artistic people in our society, is sadly underdeveloped. *Guided imagery involves using the right side of the brain to create the images and the feelings and send messages to the left side of the brain to work with it to create the changes desired.*

People often find it difficult to visualize specific images such as a field with flowers, or a beautiful full moon drifting in and out of the clouds. This is not a sign of dysfunction, but merely an indicator that practice is needed to fine tune the mind's creative abilities. Our ability to visualize effectively is not unlike learning to play an instrument. **Practice—Practice —Practice.** So be gentle with yourself and allow this to be a process, an unfolding, or even a transformation.

You can create the most magnificent scenes, of building the most magnificent mansions and traveling the most adventurous roads. Just allow it!

THE WHEN AND WHERE OF A GUIDED IMAGERY

A guided imagery produces the best results in a controlled environment. This may include dim lighting, comfortable seating, no interruptions, (no phone calls or visitors), limited outside noises and access to music/CD player/laptop or tablet. Many people find it quite helpful to accompany the verbal or mental imagery process with gentle relaxing, meditative music. If you have a prepared script, it is also helpful to record the entire session for possible re-use. You could take some of the scripts in this book and record them for your own personal use, or you can write your own scripts and record them with gentle music or ocean sounds in the background.

The best time to do a guided imagery is when you have identified a need. It is also important to have the appropriate environment and adequate time. Guided imageries can take from ten (10) to sixty (60) minutes, depending on the purpose, but it is important not to rush the process, no matter how much time you have allotted.

http://www.bing.com/videos/search?q=30-Minute+Guided+Meditation&&view=detail&mid=503A9645 69513AA2319C503A964569513AA2319C&FORM=VRDGA R "Guided Meditation and Visualization."

SOME REACTIONS DURING A GUIDED IMAGERY

During a recent training workshop in which I trained psychotherapists to use this technique, the participants experienced several different reactions as I led them through the exercises. Two therapists noted major sinus drainage occurred during one exercise, and their sinuses seemed more open and clearer afterward. One therapist "snored" loudly during one exercise, but much to the surprise of the other participants, he heard every word and followed every instruction.

These reactions are quite common and occur often during individual sessions. Other common reactions are body, arm and leg jerking, coughing, laughing, and crying. The jerking movements occur much more frequently in those who are tense and have not recently experienced a deep state of relaxation. Coughing often occurs when sinuses drain, usually as the body and all muscles and tissues experience deep relaxation. Laughing can occur as a joyous reaction to the imagery or to an interaction happening between the person and someone or something within the imagery. Laughing can also occur as a reaction the relaxation. Tears are also quite common and often indicate a deep level of relaxation has been achieved. It may even be due to a sense of relief experienced.

Some people have been known to drift "too deeply" in this relaxation exercise and go to sleep. This happens when the person goes deeper than the alpha brain wave level into theta brain wave level, a much deeper state of relaxation usually associated with the dream sleep level. I have found that doing guided imageries in the late afternoon or evening involves some risk that the client may drift deeper into the theta or sleep level. People often lay down when they do the guided imagery exercise, and their body naturally falls asleep. It would be best to sit comfortably with you head supported, but not so comfortable to go to sleep.

One way that I've learned as I guide people through an exercise is to monitor this potential sleep problem and to ask for a verbal response from the person to a question such as, "Do you see the purple flowers now?" I will just say nod your head or lift one of your fingers if you do see the purple flowers. This question and response, if given, assures me that the person is not sleeping. Another technique I use is to touch the person's hand or pat it gently when I suspect sleep and encourage the focusing on my voice.

Here is a simple 30-minute Relaxation Meditation which only plays music and has you observing kites flying in the air. It produces a calming almost hypnotic effect. Click the link or paste this into your browser.

http://www.bing.com/videos/search?q=Beginner+Meditation+30+Minutes&&view=detail&mid=564475B0441F2FDACDB3564475B0441F2FDACDB3&FORM=VRDGAR "30 Minute Relaxation Meditation."

SOME COMMON AFTER EFFECTS

There are many physical and emotional reactions which occur during and after experiencing a guided imagery. It is important to allow yourself or the person being "guided" to gently "return to the room," or regain some semblance of conscious composure. Therefore, give yourself or person being "guided" some time to chat about the experience which just took place. Allow the "cobwebs" to clear as you discuss the imagery and emotions experienced.

Quite often, people report being a little confused or foggy after an intense or long session of guided imagery. It is important to be aware of this, allow some adjustment time, and offer a word of caution about driving home. It might help to suggest a rest and relaxation period or even a bathroom break before going on to other demands of the day. *Besides feeling a little groggy, some clients report feeling sad after a guided imagery exercise.* This sadness can usually be associated with a release that occurs during the imagery and triggers a short period of grieving .This may need to be explained to the loved one so he can understand this sadness. Encourage the journaling of those feelings, if talking about them is not enough. People can be very insightful after a guided imagery, so encourage the discussion or journaling to follow the session as soon as possible.

When we release or let go of negative past experiences or emotions, we may still grieve over the loss of holding on to these feelings.

Another common feeling experienced after a guided imagery is that of relief. This is usually associated with the facing of a fear and removing its power over the person during the imagery. The relief is often experienced as a new lightness or comfort in the solar plexus area where we often store these fears. I have often heard people remark that they feel as if they just lost five (5) or ten (10) pounds. This is also a reaction to release and relief.

Many people experience exhilaration when they emerge from a guided imagery. This feeling is often associated with experiencing beautiful images and going on a "visual trip" or vacation. It is like returning from a vacation feeling exhausted, but cleansed. Another reason I feel that people feel exhilarated is the fact that they let go of conscious control for those few minutes and experience the wonderful free flow of their subconscious.

This feeling of exhilaration is often related to that of amazement at some new knowledge that is presented. This knowledge, which Bernie Siegel, MD, author of <u>Love, Medicine and Miracles,</u> refers to as "meditatively released insight," can be profound. It may take the form of a business or career decision, or may be more subtle, like a message to love oneself above all else.

Few people have guided imagery experiences that create in them a fear of participating in another guided experience. In fact, most people enjoy the experience and are often impatient to have it again.

13

IN THE BEGINNING

In order to facilitate a creative, healing experience for yourself or a loved one, many things need to be considered. First, there must be willingness. There can be little fear, as fear creates resistance. Resistance may be experienced as excessive physical movement or discomfort, or a reluctance to follow along with the initial relaxation process. Too many distracting or conscious thoughts also block the relaxation and image-making process. It is important to alleviate fear right from the start. This can be accomplished by discussing the process and stressing that the person will always be totally in control and that he/she will hear every word and remember everything that happens. Senses may be magnified, and emotions may be experienced, but they must know you will be with them and they will be safe.

Be prepared for laughter, or tears. Keep the tissue handy and put some into the person's hands if they need to wipe their eyes or nose. An emotional response can be powerful and extremely beneficial, but you must allow it to happen, and carefully monitor the persons' release.

You may find a friend or relative who can talk you through one of the following Guided Imagery Scripts. It would be most helpful if you are ill or injured to have someone lead you through one of these. If not, you may need to record the script on CD or on your laptop, or phone to play for you as you relax and follow. At the end of the handbook, there are some Websites, Links, Apps, and suggestions for other Guided Imagery Sources.

Here is a link which you can click on or paste into your browser for a unique Guided Meditation:

http://www.bing.com/videos/search?q=Guided+Imagery+Me
ditation&&view=detail&mid=43E7467F8C1D6F240AF543E
7467F8C1D6F240AF5&FORM=VRDGAR **"Guided
Mindfulness Meditation"**

A BASIC IMAGERY SCRIPT

"Find a comfortable place to relax and uncross your arms and legs.

[Start music if it is available]...

Let us begin by taking 3 slow deep breaths...

Close your eyes...Let the muscles in and around your eyes relax...

Now let that relaxation flow up to your forehead and scalp...

Now let that relaxation flow out to your cheeks and mouth and chin...

Now let that relaxation flow down from your eyes over your torso and all the way down to your feet...

Just allow that relaxation to take over your entire body now as you let go, just let go...

Now on your next few breaths exhale any remaining tension stored in any muscles or tissues or thoughts or feelings...

You may wish to scan your body, first searching for any remaining pockets of tension...and breathe that tension out on every exhale...good...

More and more relaxed with every gentle breath you take...

Now, in front of your forehead, become aware of an image screen, like a TV Screen, and on this image screen is your private showing of wonderful, healing images...

The first image I would like you to visualize is that of a very secret or special place that only you can go to ...

It may be a forest or a pond, a beach or a field, a special room, or a mountain...

Whatever it is, now become aware of the colors in your special place...

Become aware of the three dimensions all around you as you now are in your special place, relaxing more and more with every breath...

This special place is a place for you to do some inner work, some healing...

While relaxing in your special place, I am going to make some statements. As I make each statement, affirm it to be true by saying it to yourself, in your mind knowing it to be true...

There is no reason to think about these statements, just feel them...feel the opening of every cell of your being, cleansing and healing.

"Every day in every way, I am getting better and better"

"Every day I am growing to know and accept myself more and more."

"Every day I am growing to love myself more and more."

"Love is the opposite of fear, where there is fear there is no love."

"My loving thoughts chase away all fear."

Know that every cell of your body has intelligence and can open to relax, to healing and cleansing....

Become aware now of a beautiful beam of white light coming from above you…

This beam is pure white and has gentleness about it as it begins to scan the top of your head…

Let it open every cell in your head now as it scans back and forth slowly, opening and cleansing each cell of toxins, poisons and limiting past thoughts, memories and feelings…

Allow the light to do its healing…open up your cells freely and feel the cleansing take place…

Slowly now, the beam of beautiful, healing, pure white light moves down your neck and now down your torso…

Feel the cleansing and healing…allow it…encourage it!

Take your time to enjoy this cleansing and healing sensation. Notice if there is any resistance and exhale out the resistance……

[*insert any other special instructions at this point*]

COMING BACK

Now, feeling more relaxed and comfortable than you have felt in a long time, we're slowly going to come back to this room...

As I count from one to five, feel yourself becoming more aware of your surroundings...

One - two – three – become aware of the room and your body – feeling relaxed and slowly coming back to this space...

Four – feel a coolness flowing over your eyes, like they are being bathed by a nice mountain stream...

Five – eyes open, feeling relaxed and wonderful like you have just had a wonderful massage and shower. Feeling like you have just begun a beautiful new adventure in your life..."

**This is the point where a discussion would take place about the experience. Are there any insights about work, family, or health? How does the person feel physically and emotionally....?

19

AFFIRMATIONS

All our lives we have been "programmed" by parents, teachers, society, and the media and now the internet. We are taught that if we do not look, think, or act in a certain way, then we are less than perfect. If we do not use "ultra-bright toothpaste," then we will not have a great smile. If we do not wear a certain brand of clothing, then we just do not fit in. This programming reinforces our poor self-images and encourages us to believe that we are not acceptable just as we are.

An affirmation is a statement that you can make to begin reprogramming your subconscious. In the early twentieth century the French physician Emile Coue used an amazingly simple affirmation with many of his patients as a kind of prescription. He found remarkable healing took place in those who repeated this statement with belief. The affirmation he often prescribed was: **"Every day, in every way, I am getting better and better."**

The role of affirmations used in a guided imagery can be powerful. This is due to being in the very suggestible Alpha brainwave state. The affirmation begins the reprogramming or planting of the seeds for change, which are being sought after or needed to feel better about oneself.

There is usually not going to be an overnight transformation in someone's personality by saying affirmations during a guided imagery, instead the change will usually be more gradual. This may be better for the person involved, so that the adjustment to change can be accommodated. Change, after all, is one of the most difficult things for most people to deal with and accept.

When should affirmations be inserted into a guided imagery? There is no hard and fast rule for this, but perhaps the more deeply relaxed the subject is, the more amenable to suggestions in the form of affirmations that they may be. Affirmations created by the individual seem to take on a more powerful impact, but prepared affirmations are always usable and good, nonetheless.

To use an affirmation outside of the guided imagery process can also be extremely helpful in producing change. Suggested techniques for using affirmations vary, but a great many people find success by taking advantage of the more relaxed times of the day, such as the first waking hour in the morning and the last hour of the evening. You can take any affirmation that you feel comfortable with and repeat it out loud 10 times in the morning, and 10 times at night for 7 to 21 days. The more feeling you put behind the affirmation, the more powerful the change will be. Writing and saying the statement out loud together adds extra power to the reprogramming.

SAMPLE AFFIRMATIONS

An affirmation is a statement and a claim. It is a claim of ownership to whatever you say or think. Therefore, the more emotion behind the statement, the more power there is in achieving this claim. Repetition of the affirmation is also extremely important.

Every day in every way, I am getting better and better.

I am a lovable and capable person.

I believe in me.

Every day I grow to know and accept myself, more and more.

Every day I grow to love myself, as I am, more and more.

I am vibrant and creative.

I am peace-filled and healthy.

I am happy and outgoing.

I am rested and full of energy

I am a positive influence in all situations I encounter.

I project love and peace at all times today.

For the next 24 hours I will attract only positive, loving situations.

With every breath, I breathe in new life, health, and energy into my body.

MORE SAMPLE AFFIRMATIONS

Affirmations which are created by the person to receive them tend to be much more powerful. It is always helpful, though, to have a storehouse of assorted affirmations from which to choose:

HEALING

I claim my right to perfect health.

My body generates healing energy to every cell.

I have a strong desire to be vibrant and healthy.

I choose perfect health.

Every cell in my body releases the stored toxins and poisons and regenerates naturally.

STRESS

I am relaxed.

I am calm.

It is my perfect right to be tranquil and at peace with myself and with the world around me.

Every day, in every way, I grow more and more positive, calm and at peace with myself.

I allow myself to relax and be at peace.

I choose peace and tranquility.

SELF-ESTEEM

I believe in myself.

I am confident.

I like myself.

I feel good about myself.

I have faith in myself.

I am lovable

Every day I grow to love myself more and more.

BEING POSITIVE

My thoughts are positive and loving, and I am always attracting this in others.

I now accept myself and others exactly as we are.

I am beautiful and lovable and have a great deal to share with others.

My life is a series of choices and I choose only positive and loving interactions with others.

BEING CREATIVE WITH YOUR IMAGES

The emotional body of the human being is overly complex and often needs a gentle touch and a soothing voice to foster the healing process we desire. Using music enhances guided imageries for clients. The music needs to be soothing and not a familiar tune which can encourage associations with the past. Meditation music, which can be found online, in most record stores or new age bookstores, is good to use since it is not easily recognized by the conscious mind as a tune which might have some past significance.

Besides using music to enhance the guided imagery process, it is important to have a comfortable chair or lounge. When we relax, the neck muscles often let the head hang limp. This is important to consider, as a lengthy guided imagery may leave you or the person being guided with some discomfort in the neck if the head was not supported in some way.

A prepared script is okay for use in leading someone through a guided imagery if it is not "read." This means that it is important to **feel** what you are reading and let the client "buy into" your feelings.

The scripts that you do use need to be totally appropriate to the client and the needs that are being identified. To that end, it helps to be aware of materials currently on the market. Old textbooks can be another source of material. The internet is an endless opportunity to find meditations and guided imageries.

Your imagination can lead you to some wonderful images to use in the guided imagery, but don't forget that there is going to have to be some structure built in if there is going to be a purpose beyond relaxation.

Workshops, journals, magazine articles and even movies, might offer some bits of wisdom which you might incorporate into your guided imagery. An extremely popular workshop by author and consultant **John Bradshaw** that was offered around the country, deals with healing the inner child. This workshop focused on Erickson's developmental stages. It looks at unmet needs for different developmental stages and relates certain behaviors that we have today to those unmet needs. One technique that can be borrowed from this approach is that of either reliving the different developmental stages of growth in your guided imagery, or just visualizing yourself at these ages of development and meeting these unmet needs.

Another popular workshop being offered around the country is the **Silva Method**. This method tends to focus on the development of the right side of the brain through many "exercises" which can be compared to the guided imagery process. The Silva method offers basic, graduate, and advanced programs and can be found in any large city in the United States and around the world by looking in the telephone directory.

INTERACTIVE GUIDED IMAGERY

After learning, practicing, and becoming extremely comfortable with guided imagery as a valuable tool, there is another technique to master which I call an Interactive Guided Imagery. Basically, what this technique does is an extension of the guided imagery process already discussed. This process does need two people, though as one is the guide and the other is being guided.

To begin an interactive guided imagery session is no different than a regular guided imagery session. This means that we first must talk the person being guided into a very relaxed state of mind. This relaxed state of mind is often called **the Alpha state**, which refers to the brain wave frequency. Once this altered state of consciousness is achieved, the process begins. This process involves using imagery or images or visualizations which can be discussed with the person who is being guided. An example of this might be to have the person tell what colors can be seen in the field, or what the flowers look like. There is often some hesitation on the part of the person to talk, as it seems unnatural or difficult to do while in this profoundly relaxed state of mind. Gentle encouragement and patience on the part of the "guide" will be important to enable the person to feel free to talk.

The use of an interactive guided imagery can be simple and straightforward, or as complex as processing an emotion. The guide must be comfortable with the entire situation and be able to continue to make the person feel safe. I also always record these sessions and highly recommend that you do, too.

There is one, simple, interactive guided imagery that I do in my office, which can take 10 to 20 minutes to do. It is that of finding a wise animal or bird. This is done by first leading the person through the relaxation process and then getting them to visualize the first animal or bird that comes to them. (A complete script of this technique can be found at the end of this workbook.) The guide asks for a detailed description of the animal and asks if it has a name. A name makes it personal and easy for you to refer to for question. Ask the person how the animal makes him/her feel. If the feeling is unsettling in any way, then it is important to find another animal to work with.

It is hoped that the feeling the person gets, will be one of warmth, safety, peace, love, gentleness, or wisdom, etc. The process goes on to have the person ask the animal questions, one at a time. The questions are ones that you may help pose for the person being guided, but the person does not have to ask them out loud. It is important that the person tells you what response he/she gets from the animal either during the session or after the session. It may be of help to you to explain to the person at this point that the words of the animal may not be spoken and heard like a normal conversation. In fact, the message may be felt or come to the heart or the head or feel like a whisper from one side. Tell them to not question the message, just relay it to you, the guide.

At this point it is important to discuss the answer the person gets form the "wise animal." The answer may be brief and to the point, such as, "be patient, or love yourself." Even those brief answers have applications to one or more important aspects of the person's life. Therefore, ask the person how the answer fits, or what the meaning is to them. You may do this during the session or find it better to do after the session. *It may be a good practice to review the questions and answers asked and received in the imagery session after the person has "returned" to an alert conscious state of mind.*

There really is no "script" for an interactive guided imagery. There is a basic relaxation, or induction, and a process which may have standard sentences or questions.

This activity requires the guide to be on the alert for symbols, colors, words, and feelings which can be, or need to be discussed

28

during or after the imagery. A little research on dreams and symbols and colors may prove to be quite beneficial.

SOME GUIDED IMAGERY SCRIPTS

RELAXATION AND INNER CLEANSING

"Find a comfortable place to relax and make sure your arms and legs are uncrossed. Become aware of your breath, as you breathe slowly and deeply now for a few moments...

Now close your eyes, and let the muscles in and around your eyes relax... Let your eyelids relax... Let them relax so much that they will not work, even if you try. Now let that relaxation flow up to your forehead and scalp. Now let that relaxation flow out to your cheeks, and mouth, and chin...

Now let that relaxation flow down from your eyes over your torso and all the way down to your feet... Just allow that relaxation to flow over you and flow through you, relaxing every muscle, every tissue, every cell...

Ten...

Nine, feel the waves of relaxation...

Eight...

Seven, more and more relaxed with every wave...

Six...

Five, more and more relaxed...

Four...

Three, feel the waves of relaxation...

Two, deeper and deeper relaxed...

One...Extremely comfortable, very relaxed and going deeper relaxed with every gentle breath you take....

Now on your next few exhales breathe out any remaining tension you may have stored in any muscles or tissues. You may wish to scan your body first, searching for any remaining pockets of tension... more and more relaxed with every gentle breath you take...(repeat) more and more relaxed with every gentle breath you take...

Now in front of your forehead become aware of an image screen, like a computer screen or a television screen. Keeping your eyes closed now... and appearing on this image screen is your private showing of a wonderful healing image. The first image I would like you to visualize is that of a secret place, or a special place that only you can go to... It may be a forest, or a pond, a beach, or a field, a special room, or a mountain... (pause) Whatever it is is okay. Now, become aware of the colors in your special place... Become aware of the three dimensions all around you, as you are now in your special place... relaxing more, and more with every breath... This special place is a place for you to do some inner work, some healing...

While relaxing in your special place I'm going to say some statements to you, and as I say each statement, affirm it to be true by saying it to yourself, in your mind, and know it to be true....

There is no reason to think about these statements, just feel them... Feel them opening every cell of your being, cleansing and healing...

"Every day, in every way, I am getting better and better..."

"Every day, in every way, I am getting better and better..."

"Every day I am growing to know and accept myself, more and more...."

"Every day I am growing to know and accept myself, more and more..."

"Every day I am growing to love myself more and more..."

"Every day I am growing to love myself more and more..."

"Love is the opposite of fear, where there is fear there is no love..."

"Love is the opposite of fear, where there is fear there is no love..."

"My loving thoughts chase away all fear..."

"My loving thoughts chase away all fear..."

Know that every cell of your body has intelligence and can open up to relax.... to healing and cleansing... and every gentle breath takes you deeper and deeper relaxed... Every gentle breath takes you deeper and deeper relaxed.

Now be in the field... and feel the breeze blowing gently on your face... Look around and watch the butterflies dance from flower to flower...(pause) and now be one of those butterflies...(pause) Feel the freedom as you dance from flower to flower... Very good!

Now be a bird singing from a tree... (pause) and feel a song come from your heart... (pause) and now back to being you, standing in the field feeling the breeze...

At the edge of the field there is a path that leads into a forest... I would like you to take that path now... and enter the forest... And as you enter the forest you become aware of the aroma of earth, of leaves, of pine... You become aware of the stature of the trees, how strong and tall they are... And if you take the time, you can tap into that strength, into that freedom, and you can reach up like the trees do , to the sun, and to the sky... become one now with the trees...(pause)

And now walk farther along the path... and you become aware of the sound of a waterfall in the distance, and as you approach the edge of the forest and the beginning of another field, you see a beautiful waterfall ahead... and at the base of the waterfall is a wonderful pond. (pause)

I would like you to walk over now and take off your shoes and socks and put your feet into this pond... and feel the silky water... Water unlike any that you have ever touched before... This is a magical, mystical pond... A pond of healing... and cleansing... and as your feet feel the gentle caress of the water, you're aware of the tingling ... and the cleansing... (pause) Go ahead now and step all the way into the pond up to your neck... You feel your skin tingle. You feel every cell in your skin open and release toxins, release the poisons from your body... Feel your skin cleanse itself, as every cell is washed and bathed by the magical, mystical waters ...

Now be aware of this special water going over and through your body... past the skin level, into the tissues, into the muscles, into the bones, into the organs, cleansing and releasing every toxin, every poison, all the accumulations of the past...

All of this is easily released if you choose to let go... so just... let... go... and release... (pause)

Feel your lungs being bathed and cleansed and the cells renewed... Feel your sinuses being cleansed and the cells being renewed... and now become aware of your heart... and the magical, mystical waters are entering your heart, entering the bloodstream, and you feel the blood flowing with a new sense of warmth... And every artery, every vein, every capillary has been cleansed and opened and all obstructions cleared - as the water does its work, its work of love... Again, just allow it...

Now focus on the area in and around your solar plexus, where we store so many negative feelings from the past... Feel where the water is cleansing the solar plexus, and again ... just let go, just release what is stored in that area... and let the water do its work of love...(pause)

And now dive under the water, and know that you can swim with the fish and breathe the water... You can breathe the water like its air ... Feel the healing continue as you swim with the fish in the pond, and look at the bottom and see all the wondrous sights there are... (pause)

And now back to the top of the water, the surface, and near the center of the pond you see a beautiful lily pad, a very large lily pad... Climb up onto it now and let the sun warm you, and dry you... the sun can't harm you, and you won't be sunburned.

And now become aware of a beautiful beam of white light coming from the sun. This beam is pure white and has a gentleness about it, as it begins to scan the top of your head... Let it open up every cell in your head now, as it scans back and forth slowly, opening and cleansing each cell of toxins and poisons and limiting past thoughts, memories and feelings...allow the light to do its healing... open up your cells freely, and feel the cleansing take placed... Slowly now the

34

beam of beautiful healing pure white light moves down your neck...and now down your torso... Feel the cleansing and healing...(pause)

Allow it...Allow it... Encourage it... Encourage it.... All the way down to your toes now...

And now feeling a wonderful sense of oneness with nature, with this pond of magical, mystical beauty, with lily pads and with the sun, and with the forest and the field... We are going to slowly come back to the place we are in right now... and know that you can come back to this mystical pond any time you wish... All you must do is close your eyes... and then take a few deep breaths and see it on your image screen in front of your forehead...

I am going to count now from one to five... and when I say the number five your can choose to open your eyes, or you can choose to just go into a deeper state of relaxation and sleep.

One... feeling better than you have felt in a long, long time...

Two, cleansed, relieved...

Three, start becoming aware of your surroundings...

Four, feel coolness flowing over your eyes, like they are being bathed by a mountain stream...

Five, eyes open when you are ready, feeling like you have just had a wonderful massage and shower.

RELEASING LIMITING THOUGHTS/EMOTIONS

Find a comfortable place to relax and make sure your arms and legs are uncrossed... and become aware of your breathing... Now let us begin by taking three slow deep breaths...

Now close your eyes... and let the muscles in and around your eyes relax... and let your eyelids relax... let them relax so much that they will not work, even if you tried... (pause)

Now let that relaxation flow up to your forehead and scalp... Now let that relaxation flow out to your cheeks and mouth and chin... Now let that relaxation flow down from your eyes over your torso and all the way down to your feet... Just allow that relaxation to take over your entire body now... as you let go... just let go...

I'm going to count now from ten to one, and with each descending number feel a wave of relaxation flowing over you, and flowing through you... relaxing every tissue, every muscle, every cell... just let it happen.,

Ten... (pause)   **nine**, feel the waves of relaxation... **eight... (pause) seven**, more and more relaxed... **six...(pause) five**, feel the relaxation flowing over you... **four...(pause) three**, more and more relaxed... **two...(pause) one**...

Now scan your body for any remaining pockets of tension… and on your next few breaths, exhale any remaining tension stored in any muscles or tissues…Good…

More and more relaxed with every gentle breath you take… more and more relaxed with every gentle breath you take…

Now keeping your eyes closed, become aware of an image screen in front of your forehead, and on this image screen is your private showing of wonderful healing images…

The first image I'd like you to visualize is that of a very secret or special place that only you can go to … it may be a forest or a pond, a beach or a field, a special room or a mountain. Whatever it is, now become aware of the colors in your special place… (pause) Become aware of the three dimensions all around you as you now are in your special place, relaxing more and more with every breath…

This special place is a place for you to do some inner work, some healing… So, while relaxing in your special place, I'm going to say some statements to you… As I say each statement, affirm it to be true by saying it to yourself, in your mind, knowing it to be true…

There is no reason to think about these statements, just feel them, feel them opening every cell of your being, cleansing and healing…

"Every day, in every way, I am getting better and better…"

"Every day, in every way, I am getting better and better…"

"Every day I am growing to know and accept myself more and more…"

"Every day I am growing to know and accept myself more and more..."

"Every day I am growing to love myself, more and more..."

"Every day I am growing to love myself, more and more..."

"Love is the opposite of fear... where there's fear, there is no love..."

"Love is the opposite of fear... where there's fear, there is no love..."

"My loving thoughts chase away all fear..."

"My loving thoughts chase away all fear..."

Know that every cell of your body has intelligence, and can open, to relax, to healing and cleansing...

Every gentle breath takes you deeper and deeper and deeper relaxed...

Every gentle breath takes you deeper and deeper and deeper relaxed...

Become aware now, on your image screen ... a beautiful field, a large field, filled with many hot-air balloons, ready to go up and float away into the beautiful blue sky filled with fluffy white clouds... There are so many balloons that you cannot even count. You see beautiful purples, reds, blues, and yellows. You see wonderful designs on these hot-air balloons...

Now be in that field and find one balloon that especially attracts you and pick it and run over to it. Touch the basket and know that it is firmly woven and very, very safe... because you are going to get in now and go on a wonderful journey, a very safe journey, a healthy journey. So make sure you're inside, and slowly untie the ropes that are holding the balloon down to the ground... and feel the balloon lifting up, and feel your body get lighter and lighter...Now as you start lifting up into the air, going up into that beautiful blue sky...

Twenty feet up... thirty feet up... Feel the lightness in your body... and you know that you're safe... Forty feet up... Coming up to the top of the other balloons all around you, and you start slowing to about fifty feet up... and your see the beautiful colors as you are on eye level, with all of the tops of all of the other balloons...What a wondrous sight... (pause)

Now you know that you want to go higher, and higher and farther off, and take a wonderful journey in your hot-air balloon. The only way to continue the journey is to release the weights, and the weights are sandbags. They're tied along the side of the basket, so you reach over, and you grab one sandbag, and as you put it into your hand you see the word **guilt** printed on this bag... So now in the bag see an image or a vision of something that brings back a feeling of guilt to you... Something from your past, something that you've carried... you have carried this limiting feeling of guilt with you all this time. Put this feeling into the bag of sand now. Feel the feeling... And take that bag of sand and throw it over the side filled with the unresolved guilt in it... See it crash to the ground below and feel the balloon lifting higher...As you release the guilt, you climb higher, you release, you let go, and you experience more... and you feel the freedom, as the balloon climbs higher...(pause)

But there are many more bags to release because there is so much to see. So, grab another bag and this bag also says guilt on it... or **shame**... So, find an incident that brings back that feeling of guilt or shame, something from your past, and see the scene ... See the scene in this bag of sand and feel the feeling...Now take that feeling perhaps that you're experiencing right now in your solar plexus and put it in the bag of sand and throw it over the side, and see it crash into the ground below... and feel the lightness in your solar plexus, as you let go of more guilt or shame...and let the balloon lift higher... higher and higher... freer, freer to see and experience more, as you release the limiting feelings and the weight that burdens you...(pause)

And now another bag of sand says **anger** on it. And you take that bag of sand and you remember an incident that you experienced that left you with anger until you see it, and visualize it... Feel that incident, feel the anger in your solar plexus... Now put the anger from that incident into the bag of sand... and throw it over the side...and let it go... And as the bag of sand is falling, say to yourself, I let go... I let go of my anger...And see the bag of sand crash to the ground below... Now you may see another bag with anger on it...do the same thing...and let it go... (pause)

Very good! Now you feel the freedom... and the balloon is flying higher, freer... You are going over other fields and streams, but you still want to experience more... And while flying in the balloon you experience the beauty, the scenery, just like you experience life... You can see more beauty and freedom without the limitations of the sand and the weight, and you can experience more without the limitations of these feelings that you have stored, and now released...

So now take another bag of sand that says **fear** on it... and think of some fear... feel that fear that you have. Perhaps it's a fear of success, a fear of failure... whatever it is, feel the feeling in your solar plexus ... and place that into the bag of sand... and see how that scene that created fear has limited you and throw the bag of sand and fear over.... and feel the freedom as you say I let go... I let go...I let go of fear... and the bag crashes to the ground below... Now you are freer, but there's another bag with fear on it... so take this bag... and fill it with a fear that you have ...take the feeling that's in your body and put in into the bag... and throw it over, and let it go... I let go of fear ... I let go... (pause)

One more bag to release and this balloon will be flying higher and freer than it ever has before... And this bag says **hurt**...There is something in your past, perhaps a relationship difficulty, which has left you with a feeling of hurt... You can feel maybe in your chest or your heart...Take that feeling, and that scene, and that incident, and put it into the bag of sand...and throw it over the side... let it go now, and as you see it falling, falling, falling down say... I let go of hurt... I let go... and watch it crash to the ground... (pause)

Take a deep breath and feel the freedom you have, feel the freedom in your body as you release and let go of feelings that have limited you... that have burdened you... You feel the balloon fly higher and look around now with a new sense of clarity and vision, as you see distances that you never thought you could see.

As you float through clouds, and the birds come by you singing their songs of freedom... and you see mountains, fields, and rivers in the distance, ... You have a clarity and focus that is unmatched by any experience you have had before...

As we approach the end of the journey on this beautiful balloon, know that you can come to this balloon and this field and experience this freedom any time you wish... All you must do is close your eyes and visualize this field with the balloons and take another safe journey... Every time you do this exercise you'll go deeper relaxed... every time you do this exercise you'll go deeper relaxed... every time you do this exercise, you'll find yourself feeling freer, and lighter... you'll be releasing new feelings that you've stored...(pause)

And now slowly the balloon is descending to a wonderful field below... You feel it coming down, and you're very safe, and very comfortable, and you feel better than you've felt in a long, long time... Slowly coming down, and it gently touches the ground,,, and as you climb safely out of the basket you know that this is just the beginning of a wonderful journey that you've begun... and you can come back any time... (pause)

And now I'm going to count now from one to five, and when I say the number five, you can open your eyes, or you can keep them closed and go off into a deep state of relaxation and sleep.

One... Two, feeling better than you have felt in a long, long time...

Three, start becoming aware of your surroundings...

Four, feel a coolness flowing over your eyes , like they are being bathed by a mountain stream...

Five, eyes open, when you are ready... feeling like you've just had a wonderful massage and shower.

SEEKING HEALING AND GUIDANCE

Find a comfortable place to relax. Make sure your arms and legs are uncrossed. And become aware of your breathing...Now let us begin by taking three slow, deep breaths...

Now close your eyes... and let the muscles in and around your eyes relax... let your eyelids relax.... let them relax so much that they won't work, even if you tried... (pause) Now let that relaxation flow up to your forehead and scalp... now let that relaxation flow out to your cheeks and mouth and chin...now let that relaxation flow down from your eyes over your torso and all the way down to your feet... just allow that relaxation to take over your entire body now as you let go.... just let go... (pause)

I'm going to count from ten to one, and with each descending number feel a wave of relaxation flowing over you, and flowing through you, relaxing every muscle, every tissue, every thought and every feeling...

Ten....

Nine... feel the waves of relaxation...

Eight... Seven, feel the waves flowing over you...

Six... Five, more and more relaxed...

Four... Three... feel relaxing waves ...

Two... One...

Now scan your body for any remaining pockets of tension and on your next few breaths, exhale out any of that tension that is stored in any muscle or tissue that you still have... (pause)

More and more relaxed, with every gentle breath you take...

More and more relaxed, with every gentle breath you take...

Now keeping your eyes closed, become aware of an image screen in front of your forehead. On this image screen is your private showing of wonderful healing images. The first image I would like you to visualize is that of very secret or special place that only you can go to. It may be a forest, or a pond, a beach or a field, a special room, or a mountain. (pause) Whatever it is - now become aware of the colors in your special place... become aware of the three dimensions all around you, as you now are in your special place... relaxing more and more with every breath...

This special place is a place for you to do some inner work, some healing... While relaxing in your special place I am going to say some statements to you. As I say each healing statement, affirm it to be true by saying it to yourself, in your mind, knowing it to be true. There is no reason to think about these statements, just feel them, feel them opening every cell of your being. Cleansing and healing...

"Every day, in every way I am getting better and better...

"Every day, in every way I am getting better and better...

"Every day I am growing to know and accept myself more and more...

"Every day I am growing to know and accept myself more and more...

"Every day I am growing to love myself more and more...

"Every day I am growing to love myself more and more...

"Love is the opposite of fear... where there's fear there is no love..."

"Love is the opposite of fear... where there's fear there is no love..."

"My loving thoughts chase away all fear..."

"My loving thoughts chase away all fear..."

Know that every cell of your body has intelligence, and can open to relax, to healing and cleansing... Now let your conscious mind drift off, for there is no reason to think... Just feel this wonderful feeling of relaxation, and know that every gentle breath you take takes you deeper and deeper relaxed... every gentle breath you take takes you deeper and deeper relaxed... (pause)

On your image screen now, in front of your forehead, visualize a beautiful building, or a mansion. Inside this building is a wonderful lobby or foyer. Step into the lobby... it is a grand lobby; with beautiful decorations... There is no one there. At the far end of the lobby you see several elevators, and you are attracted to one set of doors... Go to those doors now... and press the down button...and as the doors open you step in. And as the doors close and you press the down button and allow yourself to go deep, deep, deep into the earth. There is only one stop, and its fifty floors down...

So feel yourself sinking deeper into your chair as you go down ten floors... deeper and deeper relaxed... twenty floors... deeper and deeper... thirty floors... let your body go... forty floors down and the elevator is beginning to slow down... fifty floors down...deeper and deeper relaxed...

The doors open slowly and... you see in front of you a beautiful silky, silvery mist. It is as if it's liquid silver and it's warm, and it comes into the elevator and caresses you. You instantly feel a feeling of peace, love, and serenity... And the silky, silvery mist seems to have life, as it gently caresses you and leads you out of the elevator and down what seems like a corridor... You know that you're deep in the center of the earth... but you're safe... and as you walk down the corridor you become aware of the smell of the earth at that very deep level... that deep dark rich smell of dirt... and you continue moving ahead, even though the silver mist doesn't allow you to see too much... (pause)

You see light coming closer and closer as you walk down the corridor, and being loved and caressed by the silky, silvery mist... The light becomes brighter to you as the mist separates and you see a beautiful cave in front of you - a large cave, the size of a football field... And everywhere you look there are crystals, beautiful clusters of crystals hanging from the top of the cave, the side and from the floor.... (pause)

And as you step into the cave you feel the power emanating from these crystals... but you are being led to the very center of the cave where there is a table. Like an operating or laboratory table... climb up on this laboratory table now and relax...just lean back and relax.... and trust that all is well, and feel the energy all around you... feel every cell open to the energy of the crystals...

Above you, you become aware of some kind of a special crystal projector, projecting lights, lights on you... now be aware of a beautiful color of **red**, bathing your entire body...and let the area around your groin absorb this color red, feel as if it's breathing in. And all the cells in that area of your body in your groin open to feel and absorb this red color… (pause) and slowly the red fades…

And now the projector is bathing you in **orange**, and your feel the orange color all over, and yet just below your navel there's an area that's going to absorb and breathe in the orange, if you let it… (pause) Breathe it in now… and feel those cells open up… good… and now slowly let the orange fade…

Now you're being bathed in **yellow**… and the area in your solar plexus is going to absorb and breathe in the yellow…and you feel every cell in your solar plexus open up to take in this wonderful color, yellow… (pause)

Now the yellow fades and **green** is the color that you are being bathed in… and the area in your heart is going to absorb and breathe in this wonderful color of green… you can feel the cells in your heart open up… and bring in this green's healing wonderful color of green…(pause)

As you let the green fade now… you are now being bathed in **blue**… a beautiful shade of blue… and the area in your throat is going to be absorbing, breathing in this blue. And the cells are going to open and absorb it…and let that area relax…(pause) …and now let the blue fade…

You are now being bathed in a shade of **deep dark indigo blue**… your entire body, and your forehead is going to absorb that color, and every cell opens up… to the healing… just relax those cells, especially in your forehead, and let the deep, dark indigo blue be absorbed… (pause)

And now let that color fade…and you are now being bathed in the last color. The color is **violet**… and your whole body is being bathed by it, but the very crown of you head is going to absorb it... bring it in, breathe it in... let every cells open up to it...(pause)

Very good... now just relax and let... the wonderful **rainbow of colors** flow from your feet all the way to the top of your head, letting the crystals increase the power of this relaxation, this cleansing, this balancing exercise... You're now going to feel the red, the orange, the yellow, the green, the blue, the dark indigo blue and the violet... slowly flowing from your feet all the way to the top of your head and back... feel the flow... and feel the balancing... ...(pause)

Now just let those colors fade... let those colors fade and sit up on the table... and somewhere there, on the floor of the cave you see a special crystal that attracts you... find the crystal and hold it in your hand...and know that this crystal has power... this crystal can help you manifest anything you desire, so take this crystal with you. Put it in your pocket and take it with you and know that this is going to be a wonderful aid for you, a help in your daily life.

Now somewhere near you, you look down and you're going to see a piece of pink crystal... it's called **rose quartz**...this rose quartz is known for its healing powers of love...I'd like you to take that pink crystal that you see now, put it in your hand and place it up next to your heart... and feel a wonderful pink bubble surround you... as you feel like you're being loved, held, and totally accepted by ten people, people who don't even know you. They accept you for who you are and love you, and they are hugging you. That is what the feeling should be like... feel it now... Feel that love... (pause)

And now take that rose quartz with you, put it in your pocket and know that any time you need a boost of love, any time you need a hug and you can't get one, just reach down into your pocket and in your minds-eye feel that rose quartz... see that pink cloud surround you, and feel the love...

48

Now off to the side of the crystal cave is a smaller cave, you can see it now... and inside you see a small fire like a campfire burning, and you know in your heart that this is a very special cave. You can feel it. You can sense it. Walk over to the cave now. It is a small cave... and you can feel the energy in there... for this is your **cave of guidance**. Within this small cave there is an energy or and entity, or a power, or a presence, and you can easily tap into energy, this presence. When you're clear, when you're centered, like you are now you can feel the presence of this power, or energy... so step into the cave now and sit down near the fire and look at the flames...and go deeper relaxed, deeper and deeper .... (pause) Now become aware of this presence near you. You may see someone, you may see something, it could be a face or a form...or you could just feel a presence. Now you have time now to ask three questions of this energy, this presence, this power... Ask three questions, and expect to get the answers... The questions can be anything about your life about which you would like to know the answers. Take your time now and know that the answers are coming... believe that the answers are there...(pause)

If the answers to your questions are not clear, then know that these answers will become clearer in the next twenty-four hours. If the answers are not what you expected... perhaps this is the time to think... Think about what the questions really that are you wished to be answered... You may come back to this cave any time and balance yourself with the colors... You can also feel the power of the crystals.... But especially you may come back and ask questions... and expect to get answers... expect to get guidance... Guidance to the questions in your life that you really wish to have answered... It is important to believe that these questions will be answered... Believe this from your heart. (pause)

Every time you do this exercise, you will go deeper relaxed. Every time you do this exercise, you will find more balancing, more healing... You will find new awareness in the cave of guidance... Every time you do this exercise there will be more power...(pause)

Slowly now, leave the small cave and thank the presence, the entity, or the power that you felt in there for the time and the answers... Again, know that you can come back... And exit slowly through the crystal cave, to the corridor with the silvery mist... Walking through the corridor again and feeling the loving caress of that silky, silvery mist...Being led to the elevator doors...and stepping in. Now feeling so balanced, so clear, and remembering that you have two crystals in your pockets...And knowing that you have the answers to some questions you wished answered. You feel that you do have now in your power a source of more answers... Slowly now the elevator starts ascending, and you can feel it going up... up ten floors. . Up twenty... Up thirty... Slowing down at the lobby... and you step out into the lobby feeling like you've just had a wonderful journey, returning refreshed, relaxed... and as I count from one to five... you have a choice of opening your eyes at the number five, or just staying in this wonderful peaceful state of relaxation, and going deeper relaxed...

One... two, feeling better than you have felt in a long, long time...

Three, start becoming aware of your surroundings...

Four, feel a coolness flowing over your eyes, like they are being bathed by a mountain stream...and...

Five, eyes open when you are ready... feeling refreshed, relaxed, like you have just had a wonderful massage and shower.

IMPROVING SELF-IMAGE

Find a comfortable place to relax, and make sure your arms and legs are uncrossed... become aware of your breath...and let us begin by taking three slow, deep breaths... Now close your eyes... and let the muscles in and around your eyes relax, and let your eyelids relax ...let them relax so much that they won't work, even if you tried...(pause) Now let that relaxation flow up to your forehead and scalp. Now let that relaxation flow out to your cheeks, and mouth, and chin... Now let that relaxation flow down from your eyes, over your torso, and all the way down to your feet. Just allow the relaxation to take over your entire body now as you let go... just let go... I am going to count from 10 to 1, and with each descending number, feel a wave of relaxation flowing over you, and flowing through you, relaxing every muscle, every tissue, every cell.

10... 9, feel the waves of relaxation...

8... 7, feel the relaxation flowing through you...

6... 5, more and more relaxed...

4...
3...
2...
1.

Now scan your body and search for any remaining pockets of tension, and on your next few breaths, exhale that tension that is stored in any muscles or tissues, exhale it right out... More and more relaxed with every gentle breath you take... More and more relaxed with every gentle breath you take... Now keeping your eyes closed, become aware of and image screen in front of your forehead, and on this image screen is your private showing of a wonderful healing image.

51

The first image I would like you to visualize is that of a very secret or special place that only you can go to. It may be a forest or a pond, a beach or a field, a special room, or a mountain. Whatever it is now become aware of the colors in your special place, become aware of the three dimensions all around you, as you are now in your special place, relaxing, more and more with every breath... (pause) This special place is a place for you to go to and do some inner work, some healing...While relaxing in your special place I'm going to say statements to you, and as I say each statement, affirm it to be true by saying it to yourself, in your mind. Know these things to be true. There is no reason to think about these statements, so let your conscious mind drift off. Just feel these statements, feel them opening every cell of your being, cleansing and healing.

"Every day, in every way, I am getting better and better..."

"Every day, in every way, I am getting better and better..."

"Every day I am growing to know and accept myself more and more..."

"Every day I am growing to know and accept myself more and more..."

"Every day I am growing to love myself more and more..."

"Every day I am growing to love myself more and more..."

"Love is the opposite of fear. Where there's fear there is no love..."

"Love is the opposite of fear. Where there's fear there is no love..."

"My loving thoughts chase away all fear..."

"My loving thoughts chase away all fear..."

Know that every cell of your body has intelligence and can open to relax for healing and cleansing... And every gentle breath takes you deeper and deeper relaxed. (REPEAT) Every gentle breath takes you deeper and deeper relaxed...

Become aware now on your image screen of a beautiful mansion, a mansion of your design. It can be one that you've seen before, or one you're creating right now... slowly approach the mansion from the front and enter the front door... and step into the foyer... the entrance of this wondrous mansion...Walk around and see the beautiful furniture, the paintings, the decorations... Become aware of a beautiful staircase leading up to the second floor... Now proceed up this staircase and know in your heart that wonderful things await you up these stairs. As you reach the top of the staircase you are aware of many doors with signs on them... The door that attracts you most is the **Relaxation Room.**

So enter into it now and see the beautiful Jacuzzi with the water gently moving. Disrobe now and step into the Jacuzzi and feel how different this water feels, so silky and soft. As it flows gently over your skin, you feel the relaxing effects on your skin and you feel your cells being cleansed, and you know now this is not ordinary water. This is magical, mystical water... and you feel the water flowing past the surface of the skin and down through the tissues, and muscles and the bones... all of your cells....Now you feel your cells being opened and cleansed of toxins and residue which are unnecessary to your wellbeing... Feel your organs being cleansed... Feel the water flowing through every part of your body. Just let go and release those toxins, those poisons, those tensions. Just exhale now and let go...(Pause)

Now relaxed and refreshed, step out of the Jacuzzi, and put your clothes back on and exit the relaxation room to the hallway. In the hallway see another room with a sign saying **Media Room.**

Enter this room now and see all the equipment. All of the equipment that you could possibly want in a mixed media room - computers, books, stereos, CD equipment, paint, easels, drawing pads, pencils, clay – everything that any artist would need to create. Look around now and add any other equipment that you would like to have... Now sit down in front of a clump of clay, or in front of an easel, or a computer, and create a 3-dimensional image of you as you would like to be. Perhaps you would like to be slimmer, or stronger, or more confident.

Create that image now... Make sure you put in every detail... including the expressions on your face... see this completed 3-dimensional you as not only a possibility of what you can become but this is who you really are underneath the layer of limiting thoughts and emotions which you have stored...(Pause) See yourself in this figure as the real you. Now take that 3-dimensional figure and add more color to the scene...turn up the light and make the image brighter... and make the whole image larger... and as you observe this real you – brighter, and more colorful – add the emotion of desire....

As you see this image, desire this image to be you. Feel that desire in your chest now. Look at the image and feel that desire. You wish to be this image. Feel it... Now add a second emotion, the emotion of belief. Believe this is really you, right now. Believe it. Feel that in your chest. Feel the belief that this is you... And now a third emotion... Add expectance. Expect this image to be the real you, right now. Expect it, just as if you were expecting a wonderful gift. For this is a gift, and you hold it within you... (pause)...Now remember this image and the three emotions of desire, belief, and expectancy. And know that *the subconscious mind does everything in its power to create what it perceives you to be, and right now it perceives you to be* this image... the more you see this image, the more powerful this image has an effect on your subconscious mind.

54

The more desire, belief, and expectancy that you have, the more power the change in you will be... now as you look at this image, say the following statements to yourself:

"I believe in myself."

"I believe in myself."

"I am capable."

"I am capable."

"I am lovable."

"I am lovable."

"I am confident."

"I am confident."

"I feel good about myself."

"I feel good about myself."

You may come back to this special mansion at any time. You may go on to the media room again and create other images. This image you see now is the real you and is manifesting right now. Come back to this room often, and every time you do this exercise, you will go deeper and deeper relaxed.

Now, slowly now, we are going to come back to this room where you are. As I count from 1 to 5, you will have a choice of opening your eyes at 5 or going on to a deeper state of relaxation and sleep.

1, feeling better than you have felt in a long, long time.

2, believing in how lovable and confident you really are.

3, start becoming aware of your surroundings.

4, feel a coolness flowing over your eyes, like, they are being bathed by a mountain stream.

5, eyes open when you are ready, feeling refreshed and relaxed, like you've just had a wonderful massage and shower.

RELEASING LIMITING THOUGHTS/EMOTIONS

Find a comfortable place to relax, and make sure your arms and legs are uncrossed...and become aware of your breathing...Now let's begin by taking three slow, deep breaths... and close your eyes... and let the muscles in and around your eyes relax, and let your eyelids relax...Let them relax so much that they won't work, even if you tried... Now let that relaxation flow up to your forehead and scalp... now let that relaxation flow out to your cheeks, and mouth, and chin... Now let that relaxation flow down from your eyes, over your torso, and all the way down to your feet. Just allow that relaxation to take over your entire body now as you let go, just let go... I am going to count from 10 to 1 now, and with every descending number, feel a wave of relaxation flowing over you, and flowing through you, relaxing every muscle, every tissue.

10... 9, feel the wave...

8... 7, feel the waves of relaxation...

6... 5, more and more relaxed...

4... 3, feel the waves of relaxation...

2... and 1.

Now scan your body searching for any remaining pockets of tension, and on your next few breaths, exhale any of that tension that is stored. Exhale the tension right out... more and more relaxed with every gentle breath you take... (repeat) more and more relaxed with every gentle breath you take... Now keeping your eyes closed, become aware of an image screen in front of your forehead, and on this screen is your private showing of wonderful healing images. The first image I would like you to visualize is that of a very secret of special place that only you can go to. It may be a forest or a pond, a beach or a field, a special room, or a mountain.

Whatever it is that you have created I want you to now become aware of the colors in your special place. Become aware of the three dimensions all around you, as you are now in your special place, relaxing, more and more with every breath... This special place is a place for you to do some inner work, some healing... So, while relaxing in your special place I am going to say statements to you. As I say each statement, affirm each to be true by saying the statement to yourself, in your mind. Know each one to be true. There is no reason to think about these statements, so let your conscious mind drift off. Just feel them, feel them opening every cell of your being - cleansing and healing.

"Every day, in every way, I am getting better and better..."

"Every day, in every way, I am getting better and better..."

"Every day I am growing to know and accept myself more and more..."

"Every day I am growing to know and accept myself more and more..."

"Every day I am growing to love myself more and more..."

"Every day I am growing to love myself more and more..."

"Love is the opposite of fear, where there's fear there is no love..."

"Love is the opposite of fear, where there's fear there is no love..."

"My loving thoughts chase away all fear..."

"My loving thoughts chase away all fear..."

Know that every cell of your body has intelligence, and can open to relax creating healing and cleansing... And every gentle breath you take takes you deeper and deeper relaxed. Every gentle breath you take takes you deeper and deeper relaxed.

On your image screen now, in front of your forehead, see or visualize a beautiful beach on a tropical deserted island... a beach that only you can go to. Now I would like you to walk along this beach and feel the sand on your feet. The sun cannot harm you. Just feel now the water, the warm water on your toes. Smell the sand, smell the salt, smell the tropical air. It is so beautiful and peaceful here. The palm trees are gently swaying in the breeze. And as you walk along the sand and the shore, you know there is nothing to worry about. You are totally at peace...

Up ahead you see an area where the water seems to jut inland a little, and as you approach closer and closer you see that there is a lagoon. It has been carved out over the years by the water. It is a beautiful lagoon - very deep. And when you get up to the edge, you see two of the most beautiful dolphins playing and swimming and jumping in the water. Leaping, and seemingly laughing, they are making their little sounds. They seem like they are dancing on top of the water. They have no fears. They have no worries. Lean over now into the water as one comes close to you. Touch its skin and feel the cool, wet skin… And as you touch the skin, allow yourself to become one with the dolphin. (pause)

Now be that dolphin … and dive into the water, and feel the coolness on your skin, and jump up into the air, and play, and laugh, and feel the freedom and the power. Feel how fast you go underwater; how high you can leap out. Jump with the other dolphin. Dive, play, swim! Now let the other dolphin swim up to you as you relax in the lagoon. The other dolphin has great wisdom to tell you… important information that you need to hear. This information is information that might change your view of life, your perspective - so that you can live life fuller, happier, more peace-filled. **Listen now as the dolphin talks to you and gives you special wisdom and guidance…**

You may wish to ask the dolphin a question or two… This dolphin is there for you any time you wish for strength, support, wisdom, and love. All you must do is close your eyes and come back to this lagoon. All you must do is believe and to know that this dolphin is the source of great wisdom and knowledge for you. Now take this knowledge and use if to benefit your life, to change your perspective, to live fuller, happier, more peace-filled… But before we leave this beautiful lagoon and beach, ask the dolphin for help: For help in releasing any emotion -- an emotion such as fear, anger, resentment, hate, envy, or guilt. These emotions have limited your progress and your ability to experience life to the fullest. Ask this dolphin what you can do

to either release the emotion or create a new perspective of it...
(pause)

Every time you come to this lagoon, you have the opportunity to learn how to release a limiting emotion - an emotion that you have stored within you instead of releasing it and experiencing the freedom from it. The dolphin has great wisdom and great guidance for you. Just be open to it, be aware, and believe it...
(pause)

Now head back to the beach and smell the salt air and bid the dolphins goodbye for now. Thank them, and bless them, and know that you will come back to this place many, many times. And every time you do this exercise, you will find yourself going deeper and deeper relaxed. Every time you do this exercise, you will feel a more profound change within you and within your life. Come back to this place often. It is a place of peace and love and healing.

And now gently coming back to place where you are now. I'm going to count from 1 to 5, and when I say the number 5, you have a choice on whether or not you want to open your eyes or remain with your eyes closed and go deeper relaxed into sleep...

1... **2,** feeling better than you have felt in a long time...

3, start becoming aware of your surroundings...

4, feel the coolness flowing over your eyes, like they are being bathed by a mountain stream...

5, eyes open when you are ready, feeling refreshed and relaxed, like you've just had a wonderful massage and shower.

FINISHING BUSINESS FROM THE PAST

Find a comfortable place to relax, and make sure your arms and legs are uncrossed... And become aware of your breathing... Let us begin by taking three slow, deep breaths... Now close your eyes... and let the muscles in and around your eyes relax, and let your eyelids relax... Let them relax so much that they will not work, even if you tried...(pause) Now let that relaxation flow up to your forehead and scalp... Now let that relaxation flow out to your cheeks, and mouth, and chin... Now let that relaxation flow down from your feet. Just allow the relaxation to take over your entire body as you let go, just let go... I am going to count now from 10 to 1, and with each descending number, feel a wave of relaxation flowing over you, relaxing every muscle, every tissue, every cell...

10...   9 feel the wave of relaxation...

8...   7, feel the relaxation flowing over you...

6...   5, more and more relaxed...

4......   3, feel that relaxation...

2...   1, very relaxed now.

Now scan your body and search for any remaining pockets of tension. If you find any tension stored in any muscles or tissues, exhale that tension on your next few breaths... More and more relaxed with every gentle breath you take... More and more relaxed with every gentle breath you take... Now become aware of an image screen in front of your forehead, and keeping your eyes closed see on this image screen your own private showing of wonderful healing images. The first image I would like you to visualize is that of a very secret or special place that only you can go to. It may be a forest or a pond, a beach or a field, a special room, or a mountain.

Whatever it is that you see, now become aware of the three dimensions all around you, as you are now in your special place, relaxing more and more with every breath... This special place is a place for you to do some inner work, some healing... While relaxing in your special place I'm going to say some statements to you, and as I say each statement, you can affirm it to be true by saying it to yourself, and in your mind know it to be true. There is no reason to think about these statements, so just let your conscious mind drift off. Just feel these statements, feel them opening and resonating in every cell of your being, cleansing and healing.

"Every day, in every way, I am getting better and better..."

"Every day, in every way, I am getting better and better..."

"Every day I am growing to know and accept myself more and more..."

"Every day I am growing to know and accept myself more and more..."

"Every day I am growing to love myself more and more..."

"Every day I am growing to love myself more and more..."

"Love is the opposite of fear, where there's fear there is no love..."

"Love is the opposite of fear, where there's fear there is no love..."

"My loving thoughts chase away all fear…"

"My loving thoughts chase away all fear…"

Know that every cell of your body has intelligence and every cell can open to relax, to healing, and to cleansing… And every time you do this exercise you are going to go deeper and deeper relaxed… Every time you do this exercise you are going to go deeper and deeper relaxed. And with every gentle breath you take, you go deeper…And with every gentle breath you take, you go deeper… (pause)

Become aware now, as you rest in your special place. Become aware of a beautiful beam of white light coming from above you. The beam is pure white and has a gentleness about it as it begins to scan the top of your head… Let it open every cell in your head now as it scans back and forth, slowly, opening and cleansing each cell of toxins, poisons, and limiting past thoughts, memories, and feelings… (pause)

Allow the light to do its healing. Open your cells freely and feel the cleansing take place… Slowly now, the beam of beautiful healing pure white light moves down your neck… And now it moves down your torso…Feel the cleansing and healing. Allow it. Encourage it…And with every breath, you go deeper and deeper relaxed… (pause) Now allow the light to fade, and let your conscious mind drift off. There is no reason to think now, just know that every time you do this exercise you go deeper relaxed… And as you focus on my voice, every word that I say takes you deeper, and deeper into a wonderful state of relaxation.

On your image screen in front of your forehead, visualize now, or see a beautiful pasture or field out in the country. See the weeds in the field gently blowing in the breeze. Feel the sun warm your skin, and know that the sun cannot harm you, because this is a magical, mystical field. This is a field of healing…(pause) Find a comfortable spot now to lie down ,

64

safely, on the field, and breath in the fresh air and go deeper relaxed...As you lie back and relax, you notice the beautiful fluffy white clouds, and the beautiful blue sky.

This is such a wonderful place of peace and serenity. You notice that each cloud that you see above has its own shape, and you are amazed as you study the clouds... And as you study them, you see one cloud take the shape of a person who was in your life. Take some time now to talk with and listen to this person and settle any unfinished business, like a negative feeling you still harbor... Perhaps you wish to forgive this person, or ask for **forgiveness** for something you've done... (pause) Now if you can, send this person love, wish them well and say goodbye, and take a deep breath and go deeper and deeper relaxed. You continue to rest in the field as you are looking up in the sky... And another cloud floats over with another face or figure from your past.

Again, this is a perfect time for you to talk with and listen to the person. Settle any unfinished business, especially unfinished business like a negative feeling that you still harbor... Perhaps you wish to forgive this person, or ask forgiveness for something you have done... If you have reached the final step of forgiveness, then it will be easy for you to send this person love... Send them a hug. Wish them well and say goodbye. And now let that person fade away, fade away... (pause)

... And go deeper relaxed as you rest in the field, as one more cloud float by. And again, it is the face or figure of someone from your past. This could be someone who may be deceased, or just geographically or emotionally removed from your life. That face is someone who does need communication with you right now so take this time to finish any unfinished business. Perhaps you wish to forgive this person or ask forgiveness for something you've done... (pause) Now wish this person well. Send love and hugs, and say goodbye, and let the person fade away... Every time you do this exercise, you will find yourself seeing people with whom you have some emotional business which is unfinished... Each time you do this exercise you will find yourself releasing stored feelings which have hindered you, and robbed you of really enjoying life... Each time you do this exercise, you release and let go of the chains that hold you to others from your past. You may find that every time you do this exercise, one person will come back many times, and that just means there is much unfinished business with that one person... So come back to the field, to **the field of forgiveness,** whenever you wish, and complete the communication, and cut those strings, and break those chains that hold you from really experiencing life to the fullest...

And now slowly, returning to this room where you are. I am going to count from 1 to 5, and when I say the number 5, you can choose to open your eyes or just drift off into a deeper state of relaxation or sleep.

1, feeling lighter, feeling better, freer than before...

2.... 3, start becoming aware of your surroundings...

4, feel the coolness flowing over your eyes, like they are being bathed by a mountain stream...

5, eyes open, feeling refreshed and relaxed, feeling lighter than before, feeling like you have just had a wonderful massage and shower.

PLANTING SEEDS FOR FUTURE HARVEST

Find a comfortable place to relax, and make sure your arms and legs are uncrossed... Become aware of your breathing...Let us begin by taking three slow, deep breaths... Now close your eyes...and let the muscles in and around your eyes relax, and let your eyelids relax...Let them relax so much that they will not work, even if you tried... Now let that relaxation flow up to your forehead and scalp... Now let that relaxation flow down from your eyes, over your torso, and all the way down to your feet. Just allow that relaxation to take over your entire body now as you let go, just let go... I am going to count from 10 to 1 now, and with each descending number, feel a wave of relaxation flowing over you, and flowing through you, relaxing every tissue, every muscle, every cell of your being...

10... 9, feel the wave of relaxation...

8... 7, feel the relaxation flowing over you...

6... 5, more and more relaxed...

4... 3, feel the wave of relaxation...

2... 1.

Now scan your body and search for any remaining pockets of tension... And on your next few breaths, exhale that remaining tension that you find stored in any muscles or tissues... good... More and more relaxed with every gentle breath you take... More and more relaxed with every gentle breath you take... Now keeping your eyes closed, become aware of an image screen in the front of your forehead, and see on this image screen your private showing of wonderful healing images.

The first image I would like you to visualize is that of a very secret or special place that only you can go to. It may be a forest or a pond, a beach or a field, a special room, or a mountain. Whatever it is, become aware of the three dimensions all around you... As you now are in your special place, relaxing more and more with every breath...This special place is a place for you to do some inner work, some healing... While relaxing in your special place I'm going to say some statements to you, and as I say each statement, affirm it to be true by saying it to yourself, in your mind, knowing it to be true. There is no reason to think about these statements, so let your conscious mind drift off. Just feel these statements, feel them opening every cell of your being, cleansing and healing.

"Every day, in every way, I am getting better and better..."

"Every day, in every way, I am getting better and better..."

"Every day I am growing to know and accept myself more and more..."

"Every day I am growing to know and accept myself more and more..."

"Every day I am growing to love myself more and more..."

"Every day I am growing to love myself more and more..."

"Love is the opposite of fear. Where there's fear there is no love..."

69

"Love is the opposite of fear. Where there's fear there is no love…"

"My loving thoughts chase away all fear…"

"My loving thoughts chase away all fear…"

Know that every cell of your body has intelligence and every cell can open to healing and cleansing and relaxation… And every gentle breath you take, takes you more and more relaxed… Every gentle breath you take, takes you more and more relaxed… (pause) Every time you do this exercise, you will find yourself going deeper and deeper relaxed…

And now become aware of your image screen again in front of your forehead… And on this image screen see a beautiful, tall building. Very tall. So tall it goes up into the clouds… And I would like you to be in front of this building and walk into the lobby and look around and see the beautiful lobby. There's no one there, just you, and you can create the lobby to be whatever you wish it to be –marble floors, tile floors, carpeted floors, deco furniture, or provincial furniture – whatever you wish. This is your lobby of your building. At the far end of the lobby is a bank of elevators, and I would like you to pick out a set of elevator doors that you are especially attracted to… Go back to those doors and press the up button. Step in when the doors open and press the up button again. This elevator goes up extremely high, but you are very safe. Very safe! There is nothing to fear.

So just relax and let your body float as you go 10 floors up… Very safe… 20 floors up… Higher… 30… 40... Just let every limb lighten up and float… 50…60… 70... Feel yourself floating... 80… 90... More and more relaxed and lighter and lighter, as the elevator's starting to slow down... Slowing down...And at 150 floors up, it stops. The doors open and you are greeted by a wonderful silky, silvery mist. A mist like liquid silver, except it is deceivingly warm and gentle, and the minute the mist touches your skin you feel loved. Allow the mist to caress you and lead you out onto what you think may be the roof of a building... But what you find is another world, another place, a very safe, loving, peaceful place... And all you see now is mist all around you, and yet the floor feels solid, and you feel so safe, so loved, and so peaceful here. This mist leads you now to a special sofa, designed so that you can view a viewing screen. The screen is like a movie screen that comes down through the mist. It is in front of you and slightly above eye level.

So, lie down now on this special sofa and be prepared to view some interesting scenes. These are scenes about you. The screen only shows scenes of incidents where you are angry or depressed, sad, lonely, fearful, tired, financially insecure, or some other limiting aspect of your behavior... Now, on the screen as it appears in front of your forehead through the mist, let a scene unfold. Let it be a scene of a behavior which you do not wish to have anymore. This is a scene from your past. See the details in the scene, the colors, the sounds, the smells, and the sizes.

See the expression on your face and the faces of those around you. See the body language; hear the words that are being said... Feel the feelings, the anger, the sadness, the loneliness, and the fear... Now allow the color that you are seeing to slowly fade into black and white... And now the scene grows slowly out of focus and shrinks down...The scene is shrinking now... Smaller and smaller the scene shrinks - until it is the size of a dot... And magically from this dot see a beautiful color scene develop on the viewing screen in front of you. This color scene shows you as you would like to act or react. It shows a balanced, healthy, functional you.

See the colors vividly. See the three dimensions. See the shapes and the sizes. See the expressions on your face and others. See the body language. And feel the warm feeling within you, now, as you see yourself functioning in this new, unlimited way... Now take this scene from the viewing screen and put it into your hand and get up from the comfortable sofa. Walk a few feet in the silvery, silky mist... See in front of you a beautiful garden. It is a garden of crystals. This crystal garden is a powerful place to plant and grow anything you desire. You now desire to have this new behavior that is on the image in your head... Take that image now and plant it under some of the beautiful quartz crystals. Quartz crystals power many things today, from watches to much of the equipment in our space shuttles. So, let the power of these crystals take this seed that you have planted. Let the crystals take this scene of what you really want in your life. Let the crystals take that scene and bring it into reality now.

Feel the power of the crystals fertilizing this image. And now step back and know that you have created the beginning of a new you. Believe that this scene is growing into reality even now. Believe it... Take some time now to visualize two or three things that you wish to attract into your life. Things like health, prosperity, more business, a loved one, success, or whatever you wish to attract. See the scene of that new manifestation in your head. See all the colors. See each scene in great clarity, and then plant it in the crystal garden. Take time to do that right now... (pause)

Know that these things that you desire and that you visualize are coming into reality, even now. They are growing into reality in the crystal garden inside of you. And the crystal garden is fertilized with the power of the crystals. But you are also fertilizing these desires with your belief, with your belief that is manifesting right now... also fertilized with your desire to have these things. And fertilized with your expectancy, your expectancy of the wonderful result. Every time you come to this garden, plant new things; new things you wish to attract into your life... Do not dig up the old things. Let the new things grow. Let them manifest - as they are now manifesting.

Every time you come to this place; you will feel the power of the garden. You will feel the power of the image on the screen that moved down through the mist into the crystals to create; to create and manifest new things into your life, and to rid yourself of those limiting feelings... Now, let us leave the garden and go back into the mist... in the silvery, silky mist to the elevator. Know that you can come back at any time, and as slowly the elevator descends... slowly descending. And you are extremely comfortable and very safe. You feel a sense of excitement in you; knowing that wondrous new things are happening within you and around you. Even now these seeds are growing, growing in your crystal garden, soon to be manifested in your life. The elevator doors open at the lobby, and I will be counting now from 1 to 5.

When I say the number 5, you can choose to open your eyes or leave them closed and go deeper into relaxation or sleep.

1... 2...

3... start becoming aware of your surroundings...

4... feel the coolness flowing over your eyes, like they are being bathed by a mountain stream...

5... eyes open when you are ready, feeling refreshed and relaxed, feeling a sense of expectancy... feeling like you've just had a wonderful shower and massage.

AN INTERACTIVE GUIDED IMAGERY SCRIPT

This is a guided imagery script which you can use to lead someone else on a journey. This is a script that you would use once they have been relaxed, using an induction of your choice. The interesting part of this script is you will have the relaxed person talk to you about what he or she is experiencing. Talking is sometimes difficult is someone is very relaxed. So, you may have to strain your hearing a bit to hear the person answer your questions.

FINDING YOUR WISE ANIMAL

(Begin this experience by using a relaxation induction of your choice. You do not have to take the client to a special place or do affirmations. In other words, just relax the client and begin this dialogue…)

"You are very relaxed now and every breath you take takes you deeper and deeper relaxed… (Repeat) …every breath you take, takes you deeper relaxed…

74

And now as you relax more and more with every word that I say, I would like you to listen to what I am saying. You do not have to think about what I am saying, just listen. There is no reason to think now, so tell your conscious mind to relax and go away as you now relax more and more...

In a moment I am going to ask you to visualize or see something in front of your forehead on your image screen. Do not think about what I am going to ask you to visualize. Just let the image appear naturally and comfortably...

Now I would like you to see or visualize the first bird or animal that comes to your mine ... do not question what you see, just let the image become clearer and clearer.

Do you see a bird or an animal now?... (Let them answer you)

Can you tell me something about your animal? What is it?... (Let them answer you)

Tell me about its size and shape...(Let them answer you)

As you look at your animal, what feeling, or feelings do you get?... (Let them answer you)

Does your animal have a name?... (Let them answer you)

Now we are going to ask your animal some questions, because it is a wise animal and it can really be of great help to you... Let us start by asking the animal if you need to do anything to correct or **prevent a physical health problem?** You may get a response which you will hear with your ears, your mind, your heart, or a whisper that comes from somewhere outside of you.

Ask the animal and just listen now and tell me what response you get... (Listen to the answer)

75

Now let us ask about some questions you may have about relationships, job, money"… (Listen to the answers)

(During these questions it is important to carefully listen to answers given and see if they need to be clarified or discussed while in this relaxed state, or if you should wait until the imagery session is over. You also may ask the person what his/her reaction is to the answer given to any of the questions. Sometimes the discussions that are held while in this relaxed state can be quite beneficial… when you have asked enough questions, prepare to bring the person back…)

"Now, listen as I tell you that this wise animal is always going to be available to you. From now on, all you must do to contact your wise animal is to close your eyes, relax and clear the clutter of the day. Use your wise animal as a sounding board to get an opinion about some decision you need to make. Your wise animal may even appear in your dreams now, giving you advice, sometimes hidden in symbols, or giving you a realistic scene to consider.

And now I am going to count from 1 to 5 and when I say the number five, you will open your eyes.

One… feeling better than you have felt in a long, long time…

two, cleansed, relieved…

three, start becoming aware of your surroundings…

four, feel a coolness flowing over your eyes, like they are being bathed by a mountain stream…

five, eyes open, when you're ready, feeling like you've just had a wonderful massage and shower."

CONCLUSION

Guided Imagery is a technique to take you away from your busy, problem-solving, worrying mind. It takes you to a place where you can escape and find peace and quiet, healing and miracles, wonder and joy. It is a magical journey with endless possibilities as to where you might end. Guided Imagery is used to help athletes visualize themselves performing the correct movements. It is used by stressed people to reduce stress. It is used by ill people to enhance the healing process. It is used by creative people to help "see" what their next creation or project might be. As we have said before - the uses of doing Guided Imagery are endless.

Learning this process just takes time and practice, and perhaps a little guidance. If this is your first exposure to Guided Imagery, please do not give up if your mind is too busy to let you experience the visuals. Keep trying! This is a gift that will change your life. The most difficult thing for most people is setting aside the time to give themselves the gift of doing a Guided Imagery. So that is the challenge to you. Look at your schedule and see where you can allow yourself 15 or 20 minutes, 2 or 3 times a week. Pick a Guided Imagery online that has what you are looking for. (For example: relaxation, building self-esteem, or cleansing the busy mind) Make sure that you like the voice of the person who leads you through the session, as it should be soothing to you. Turn off your phone, and the television nearby. Find a quiet, comfortable place, and let yourself soar.

APPS

http://www.healthline.com/health/mental-health/top-meditation-iphone-android-apps "The best meditation apps of 2016."

http://www.mindful.org/free-mindfulness-apps-worthy-of-your-attention/ "Free Mindfulness Apps worthy of your attention."

http://www.gearbrain.com/vr-apps-virtual-reality-meditation-yoga-mobile-headset-1873315555.html

"7 best VR meditation apps for mobile-based headsets."

https://www.headspace.com/headspace-meditation-app "Headspace app."

https://play.google.com/store/apps/details?id=com.getsomeheadspace.android&hl=en "Headspace-meditation."

https://play.google.com/store/apps/details?id=com.bmt&hl=en "Buddhist Meditation Trainer."

http://www.wired.com/2016/04/meditation-apps-iphone-android/ "Great meditation apps that'll help keep it together."

http://www.vogue.com/13276498/best-meditation-apps-mindfulness/ "7 meditation apps to try now."

http://www.lifehack.org/articles/technology/12-iphone-apps-for-meditation.html "12 iPhone apps for meditation."

http://www.digitaltrends.com/mobile/best-meditation-apps/

"A beginner's guide to mindfulness meditation, and the best apps for learning."

YOUTUBE VIDEOS

http://www.bing.com/videos/search?q=guided+imagery+yout ube&qpvt=guided+imagery+youtube&FORM=VDRE_ "A general selection of Guided Imageries on YouTube."

https://www.youtube.com/watch?v=1vx8iUvfyCY "Guided Meditation for Detachment from Over-Thinking."

https://www.youtube.com/watch?v=8_jcEpwKQXc "Guided Meditation – Anxiety Relief"

https://www.youtube.com/watch?v=6vO1wPAmiMQ "Guided Meditation for Anxiety & Stress, Beginning Meditation, Guided Imagery Visualization"

https://www.youtube.com/watch?v=oJjc4XreJSQ "GUIDED SLEEP TALKDOWN - GENTLE RAIN. 1 HOUR. Insomnia and Relaxation."

https://www.youtube.com/watch?v=o0EQEiecSxs "Positive Thinking Meditation: Endorphin Meditation with Positive Affirmations"

https://www.youtube.com/watch?v=EPWpV064K24 "GUIDED MEDITATION - Clearing Negativity"

https://www.youtube.com/watch?v=ar_W4jSzOlM "Ocean Escape (with music): Walk Along the Beach Guided Meditation and Visualization"

https://www.youtube.com/watch?v=xOVGPID8F7M "GUIDED MEDITATION for Healing, Energy & Enlightenment"

https://www.youtube.com/watch?v=e33dETmxAr0 "GUIDED MEDITATION - Blissful Inner Peace" https://www.youtube.com/watch?v=N4qCFFBrrgk "Guided Meditation for Sleep... Floating Amongst the Stars"

https://www.youtube.com/watch?v=k_bHsDSuoP0 "Meditation for Depression."

https://www.youtube.com/watch?v=1vx8iUvfyCY "Guided Meditation for Detachment from Over-Thinking."

http://www.bing.com/videos/search?q=YouTube+Guided+Imagery+&&view=detail&mid=43E7467F8C1D6F240AF543E7467F8C1D6F240AF5&FORM=VRDGAR "Guided Mindfulness Meditation: Relaxing..."

LINKS, WEBSITES AND ARTICLES

Meditation Oasis Website for Information and Select Meditations: http://www.meditationoasis.com

Many Guided Imagery Scripts and Articles—Just type in "Guided Imagery" in the Search Box: www.Ehow.com

Article: "Guided Imagery"
http://www.Livestrong.com/article/164001-visualization-guided-imagery/

http://www.bing.com/videos/search?q=YouTube+Guided+Imagery+Grief+and+Loss&&view=detail&mid=29AB532EB1EB91C9657729AB532EB1EB91C96577&FORM=VRDGAR
"Reducing Stress"

http://www.bing.com/videos/search?q=YouTube+Guided+Imagery+Grief+and+Loss&&view=detail&mid=7E22D7A264931295CEE47E22D7A264931295CEE4&rvsmid=BB705004625410E39BDDBB705004625410E39BDD&fsscr=-2970&FORM=VDFSRV **"What is Mantra Meditation?"**

http://www.bing.com/videos/search?q=YouTube+Guided+Imagery+Grief+and+Loss&&view=detail&mid=5A8A59B5D5092F3720C45A8A59B5D5092F3720C4&rvsmid=BB705004625410E39BDDBB705004625410E39BDD&fsscr=-2970&FORM=VDFSRV **"5 of the Best Sleep Guided Meditations."**

http://www.bing.com/videos/search?q=YouTube+Guided+Imagery+&&view=detail&mid=42EA2FE91EC384C9D56042EA2FE91EC384C9D560&rvsmid=43E7467F8C1D6F240AF543E7467F8C1D6F240AF5&fsscr=-5940&FORM=VDFSRV
"15 Minute Guided Imagery Meditation Exercise."

http://www.bing.com/videos/search?q=30-Minute+Meditation+Script&&view=detail&mid=F12576F68CAEF89ECB57F12576F68CAEF89ECB57&FORM=VRDGAR "Guided Meditation: 30 minutes."

http://www.bing.com/videos/search?q=12+Minute+Meditation&&view=detail&mid=F57B249777B81E38B273F57B249777B81E38B273&FORM=VRDGAR "12 minute Relaxation Meditation."

If you feel that others would benefit from reading this handbook, please return to <u>Amazon</u> where this was purchased and <u>write a REVIEW</u>. You may also LOAN it out to a friend from that site, if you know your friend's email address.

Thank you,

RLT Publishing

BOOKS AND E-BOOKS BY RLT Publishing

"Overcoming Anger in Teens and Pre-Teens: A Parent's Guide"

"Tragedy, Trauma and Loss in Teens and Pre-Teens: Healing the Emotional Wounds"

"Overcoming Drug and Alcohol Problems in Teens and Pre-Teens: A Parent's Guide"

"Overcoming ADHD in Teens and Pre-Teens: A Parent's Guide"

"Overcoming Anxiety in Teens and Pre-Teens: A Parent's Guide"

"Overcoming Depression in Teens and Pre-Teens: A Parent's Guide"

"Overcoming Obesity in Teens and Pre-Teens: A Parent's Guide"

"Overcoming Self-Esteem Problems in Teens and Pre-Teens: A Parent's Guide"

"Senior Moments: A Guide for Aging Safely and Gracefully"

"Say What: Suggestions on What to Say in Almost Every Difficult Situation"

"Tech Etiquette: OMG"

"Guided Imagery"

"Gay Men's Guide to Love and Relationships"

"Sexual Identity? Moving from Confusion to Clarity"

"The Traveling Parent"

"Validation Addiction: Please Make Me Feel Worthy"

"Addiction in the LGBTQ Community"

"Addicted Physicians: Healing the Healer"

"Addicted Nurses: Healing the Caregiver"

"Addicted Pilots: Flight Plan for Recovery"

"Addicted Pharmacists: Healing the 'Medicine Man'"

"Tragedy, Trauma and Loss: Healing the Emotional Wounds"

SELF-ESTEEM ENHANCERS...

These Self-Esteem Enhancers are actually "affirmations" which are deeply rooted in history....

The theory is that we have become programmed by parents, siblings, society, television, the internet, the media, etc., and this programming has led to our attitudes about ourselves and others. This programming is very often negative, leaving us with a negative self-image.

By taking a positive statement, such as a Self-Esteem Enhancer attached, and repeating it for 7 to 21 days, we begin to change that programming. The more we repeat the statement, and the more feeling behind it, the stronger and quicker the results.

Thinking the statement, you pick for 10 times each day is okay, saying it out loud 10 times is good, and saying out loud it and writing it 10 times daily is excellent. One way to begin reprogramming yourself is to mentally repeat the Self-Esteem Enhancer as many times as you can during the day when you have a few free minutes.

****

Directions: Say the Self-Esteem Enhancer which you choose, 10 times in the morning just after rising, and 10 times in the evening just before bed for 7 to 21 days. Say it out loud if possible. Looking in a mirror while saying it, gives extra power to the activity. Also, the more times you say it, the quicker and more powerful the results. Concentrate on one Self-Esteem Enhancer at a time for best results. Also, do not share your Self-Esteem Enhancer with anyone else, as you don't want any chance of someone's negative thoughts or comments weakening your efforts to make a positive change in yourself. Good Luck and

Bon Voyage on your journey to loving yourself more completely..........

My life is a series of choices and I choose only positive and loving interactions with others.

For the next 24 hours I will attract only positive, loving situations.

The negativity of others bounces off me and I remain centered, focused, and clear.

I love my mind and my body.

I leave my negative self-image behind me and see only a positive love-filled me.

Others are attracted to my loving, peaceful nature. I radiate contentment.

My loving thoughts chase away all fear.

I easily release all anger in an appropriate way.

I release and let go of any need to feel guilty.

I radiate peace and contentment.

I forgive myself for living in shame and guilt and easily release the need to feel these limiting feelings.

I release those who I feel have limited or victimized me, by understanding, loving, and forgiving them.

I choose peace, love, and joy as my companions today.

The child within me plays in the moment and experiences freedom and joy.

This is my day to feel peace, love, and harmony in all that I say and do.

I deserve to experience peace, love, and harmony.

I am worthy of love.

I am honest, open, and loving in all that I say and do.

I believe in ME!

I like myself.

I am loveable.

I feel good about myself.

I have faith in myself.

I love myself.

I am confident.

I now accept myself and others exactly as we are.

Every day I grow to love myself more and more.

I believe in myself.

My thoughts are positive and loving, and I am always attracting this in others.

I am beautiful and loveable and have a great deal to share with others.

Every day, in every way, I grow more and more positive, calmer and at peace with myself.

I am a positive influence in all situations I encounter.

I am lovable and capable.

The child within me finds healthy ways of play and self-expression.

I believe in ME!

I allow myself to relax and be at peace.

I am a positive influence in all situations I encounter.

I am positive and loving.

I am source of great joy and creativity.

Every day I grow to know and accept myself more and more.

I am beautiful and lovable and have a great deal to share with others.

Every day, in every way, I am getting better and better.

ABOUT THE AUTHOR

<u>Dr. Richard Travis</u> is a Psychotherapist who is in Private Practice in Fort Lauderdale, Florida. In his psychotherapy practice, he has worked with general issues in the population, such as depression, anxiety, and relationship problems. He has also worked with a great many gay men and the HIV population for over twenty (25) years. His specialty in Addictions has allowed him to see how addictions have complicated and destroyed relationships, ruined people's health, and made chaos of their financial situations.

He received his first master's degree at Edinboro University of Pennsylvania in Education. He received his second master's degree in Counselor Education at Florida Atlantic University in Boca Raton, Florida. He received his Doctorate in Higher Education/Counseling Psychology at Florida International University in Miami, Florida. He has Specialties in Addictions, including State, National and International certifications. He has worked with several people in the healthcare industry who have been in Addiction Monitoring Programs, and currently facilitates several groups a month with professionals being monitored by state and federal agencies.

Dr. Travis has taught classes with every age level of student in Pennsylvania, Michigan, and Florida, including teaching graduate Social Work classes at Florida International University in Miami. He has also published several articles on the website Ezinearticles.com.

Printed in Great Britain
by Amazon